PARIS TRAVEL GUIDE 2023 (TEENS)

Insider Handbook Guide to Ancient History, Art, Culture, and Hidden Gems – Explore The City And Create Lasting Memories!

By

JEFF RICHY

Table Of Content

Chapter 5: Maps, Accommodations, and Transportation Tips

- Navigating Paris with Maps and Transport
- Understanding the Paris Metro
- Helpful Maps and Navigation Apps

5.2 The Perfect Place to Stay: Hotels, Airbnb, and More

- Teen-Friendly Accommodations in Paris
- Unique Farmhouse Stays near the City

Chapter 6: Activities to Make Your Parisian Adventure Unforgettable

- Hands-On Experiences and Workshops
- Art Classes and Craft Workshops
- Cooking Lessons: Mastering French Cuisine

6.2 Enjoying the Outdoors: Parks, Gardens, and Picnics

- Relaxing in Parisian Parks
- Scenic Picnic Spots with a View

Chapter 7: Language and Travel Essentials

- Bonjour! Basic French for Your Parisian Adventure
- Handy Phrases for Getting Around
- Polite Expressions and Greetings

7.2 Best Travel Season and Packing Tips

- Dressing for Different Seasons
- Packing Light for Easy Exploration

Introduction

This handbook is your ultimate companion for exploring the magical world of Paris, designed especially for young adventurers like yourself. In the following pages, we'll embark on a thrilling journey through the heart of this iconic city, unraveling its rich history, savoring its vibrant culture, and uncovering its hidden treasures.

From the majestic Eiffel Tower to the awe-inspiring Louvre, we'll take you on a whirlwind tour of Paris's most famous landmarks. But that's not all; this guide goes beyond the tourist hotspots to reveal lesser-known spots adored by locals, ensuring you get a taste of authentic Parisian life.

As we delve into the city's captivating history, you'll learn how Paris has shaped the world of art, literature, and fashion. With a wealth of information on local customs and dining etiquette, you'll feel like a true Parisian during your stay.

Whether you're an art enthusiast, a history buff, a foodie, or simply an adventurer seeking new experiences, "Paris Unveiled" has something special for everyone. Prepare to be captivated by the allure of this mesmerizing city and create memories that will last a lifetime.

So, fasten your seatbelts, and get ready for an unforgettable journey through the City of Lights. Paris is waiting to be unveiled, and we can't wait to share this extraordinary adventure with you. Let's explore Paris together and make this trip one you'll cherish forever!

Chapter 1
Unraveling Paris's History, Cultural Heritage, and Art

Welcome to the captivating realm of Paris, where history, cultural heritage, and art intertwine to create a city like no other. In this chapter, we will embark on an immersive journey through time, exploring the tapestry of Paris's past, understanding the profound influence of French history, and embracing the local traditions and customs that make this city so enchanting.

Discovering the Rich Cultural Heritage of Paris

Paris stands as a living testament to the various civilizations that have graced its land throughout the ages. From its humble beginnings as a settlement of Celtic tribes called the Parisii to its rise as a powerful Roman city known as Lutetia, Paris has undergone a remarkable transformation over thousands of years.

As we wander through the cobblestone streets, we encounter the remnants of medieval Paris, a time when grand cathedrals and churches were constructed, each a masterpiece of Gothic architecture. The iconic Notre-Dame Cathedral, with its stunning flying buttresses and intricate stained-glass windows, serves as a timeless symbol of the city's devotion to faith.

Another pivotal era in Parisian history was the Renaissance, a period of intellectual and artistic reawakening. It was during this time that art flourished, and the city became a haven for painters, sculptors, writers, and philosophers. The influence of Renaissance art is evident in various museums and galleries, showcasing the works of geniuses like Leonardo da Vinci and Michelangelo.

The 18th century saw the rise of Paris as the center of the Age of Enlightenment, where new ideas and philosophies reshaped the city's landscape. The French Revolution, a defining moment in history, further solidified Paris's significance on the world stage, as the ideals of liberty, equality, and fraternity resonated far beyond its borders.

Understanding the Influence of French History

The history of Paris is deeply intertwined with the history of France, a country that has played a crucial role in shaping the world's politics, arts, and culture. From the reign of influential monarchs like Louis XIV, the "Sun King," to the tumultuous periods of revolution and upheaval, each chapter of French history has left a lasting imprint on the identity of Paris.

The Palace of Versailles, a short distance from the city, is a testament to the grandeur and opulence of French royalty. The lavish gardens, the Hall of Mirrors, and the king's apartments offer a glimpse into the extravagant lifestyle of the French monarchy.

Embracing Local Traditions and Customs

Parisians hold their cultural traditions dear, and as visitors, immersing ourselves in these customs allows us to connect with the heart and soul of the city.

The Parisian lifestyle revolves around the joy of savoring delectable food and spending leisurely afternoons at charming cafes. From buttery croissants to rich escargot, the French cuisine is a delightful adventure for the taste buds. As we explore the city's vibrant markets, we discover the importance of fresh produce and local ingredients in French gastronomy.

One of the most cherished Parisian customs is the art of "flânerie," which refers to taking leisurely strolls through the city streets, observing life as it unfolds. This tradition allows us to appreciate the city's beauty at a leisurely pace, from the majestic architecture to the ever-changing Seine River.

Moreover, the French language is an integral part of Parisian culture. While the thought of speaking French might seem intimidating, a few simple phrases go a long way in building connections with the locals and expressing our respect for their culture.

Unraveling Paris's History, Cultural Heritage, and Art

Welcome to the mesmerizing world of Paris, where history, cultural heritage, and art intertwine to create an extraordinary tapestry that has captivated hearts for centuries. In this chapter, we embark on an immersive journey through time, delving deep into the fascinating past of Paris, understanding the profound influence of French history, and embracing the local traditions and customs that lend the city its unique charm and allure.

Discovering the Rich Cultural Heritage of Paris

As we venture into the enchanting streets of Paris, we are transported back in time, witnessing the layers of history that have shaped this iconic city. Paris, originally known as Lutetia, was established as a humble settlement of Celtic tribes called the Parisii around 250 BC. Over the centuries, it evolved into a thriving Roman city, known as Lutetia Parisiorum, and its position on the Seine River made it a strategic center for trade and commerce.

The medieval period left an indelible mark on Paris, as grand cathedrals and churches adorned the cityscape. The Notre-Dame Cathedral, a masterpiece of Gothic design, stands as a testament to the city's devotion to faith and architectural brilliance. Its soaring spires, intricate rose windows, and majestic interiors continue to awe visitors, exemplifying the beauty and craftsmanship of the Middle Ages.

The Renaissance era brought forth a cultural renaissance in Paris, with art, literature, and science flourishing. The city became a hub for intellectuals, artists, and visionaries from across Europe. The likes of Leonardo da Vinci, who spent his final years in France, and Michelangelo left an indelible imprint on the city's art scene, and their masterpieces can be admired in the Louvre and other renowned museums.

The Age of Enlightenment, during the 18th century, marked a period of intellectual awakening and social transformation. Ideas of reason, individual rights, and democracy took center stage, and Paris became a hotbed of philosophical discussions and debates. The French Revolution, which began in 1789, forever altered the course of Paris and France, making it a symbol of liberty, equality, and fraternity.

Understanding the Influence of French History

The history of Paris is inseparable from the history of France, a nation that has played a pivotal role in shaping the world's politics, arts, and culture. Paris served as the seat of power for the French monarchy, witnessing the reigns of illustrious monarchs like Louis

XIV, known as the "Sun King," and Louis XVI, whose reign culminated in the French Revolution.

The Palace of Versailles, located a short distance from Paris, stands as a testament to the grandeur and opulence of the French monarchy. Originally a hunting lodge, King Louis XIV transformed it into an extravagant palace that became the center of political and social life in France. The opulent Hall of Mirrors, the royal apartments, and the stunning gardens are a vivid reflection of the lavish lifestyle of the kings and queens of France.

During the French Revolution, Paris became the epicenter of radical political and social change. The storming of the Bastille on July 14, 1789, marked the beginning of a tumultuous period that would reshape the course of history. The Revolution gave birth to new ideas of governance and led to the rise of Napoleon Bonaparte, whose reign brought both military conquests and cultural transformations.

Embracing Local Traditions and Customs

Parisians take immense pride in their cultural heritage, and as visitors, immersing ourselves in their customs allows us to connect with the heart and soul of the city.

The Parisian lifestyle revolves around savoring delectable food and indulging in leisurely moments at charming cafes. French cuisine is a delightful adventure for the taste buds, with its rich flavors, delicate pastries, and diverse regional specialties. The bustling street markets, such as Marché Bastille and Marché des Enfants Rouges, offer a feast for the senses, with fresh produce, artisanal cheeses, and aromatic spices.

One of the most cherished Parisian customs is the art of "flânerie," which refers to taking leisurely strolls through the city, observing life as it unfolds. This cherished tradition allows us to appreciate the city's beauty at our own pace, from the majestic architecture to the ever-changing Seine River. It is a moment of contemplation, an opportunity to observe the vibrant street life, and a chance to connect with the rhythm of Parisian life.

The French language is an integral part of Parisian culture, and while fluency may seem daunting, a few simple phrases go a long way in building connections with the locals. A friendly "Bonjour" or "Merci" not only brightens someone's day but also showcases our respect for the local culture and a genuine effort to connect.

1.2

Exploring the Artistic Treasures of Paris

Paris, a haven for art enthusiasts, holds a wealth of artistic treasures that span centuries and genres. In this chapter, we embark on an enthralling journey through the city's renowned art museums and galleries, where masterpieces from the world's greatest artists await to captivate our senses and ignite our imagination.

The World-Famous Louvre: An Art Lover's Dream

The Louvre, an iconic symbol of Paris, stands majestically on the right bank of the Seine River, welcoming millions of visitors each year. This colossal former royal palace houses an incomparable collection of art that spans over 9,000 years of human history. As we step inside the Louvre's grand courtyard, the Cour Carrée, we find ourselves at the heart of a cultural marvel that houses over 380,000 objects, from ancient artifacts to Renaissance paintings and beyond.

Navigating through the Louvre can feel like embarking on a treasure hunt, with each room revealing a new gem. In the Egyptian Antiquities section, we encounter awe-inspiring sculptures, such as the Sphinx of Tanis and the monumental statue of Ramses II. These artifacts offer a glimpse into the grandeur of ancient civilizations that once flourished along the Nile.

The Louvre's vast collection of European paintings takes us on a journey through artistic evolution. We marvel at Leonardo da Vinci's enigmatic masterpiece, the Mona Lisa, with her enigmatic smile capturing the imagination of visitors from around the world. Nearby, we find the majestic painting of Liberty Leading the People by Eugène Delacroix, a poignant symbol of the French Revolution and its enduring spirit.

Moving through the galleries, we encounter captivating works by the Flemish and Dutch masters, such as Vermeer's ethereal The Lacemaker and Rembrandt's introspective self-portraits. In the Italian Renaissance wing, Raphael's The Wedding of the Virgin and Titian's Bacchus and Ariadne grace the walls, showcasing the brilliance of human creativity during this transformative period.

For sculpture enthusiasts, the Louvre's collection is a treasure trove of masterpieces. A beautiful sculpture of Nike from the Hellenistic period known as the Winged Victory of Samothrace stands with its wings outstretched, conjuring up images of triumphant motion preserved in stone. In contrast, Michelangelo's captivating Slaves seem to emerge from their marble prisons, embodying the struggle between the artist's vision and the raw material.

Beyond European art, the Louvre's Islamic Art and Decorative Arts sections offer insights into other rich artistic traditions. The intricately designed tiles, textiles, and ceramics display the cultural diversity and ingenuity of civilizations across time.

Masterpieces of the Musée d'Orsay

Housed in an elegant former railway station, the Musée d'Orsay is a treasure trove of 19th and early 20th-century art. This exceptional collection showcases the artistic innovations and revolutions that occurred during this transformative period.

As we step into the grand nave of the museum, we are immediately struck by the beauty of the space and the impressive clock at the far end, which offers a panoramic view of the Seine River and the city beyond.

The Musée d'Orsay boasts an extensive collection of Impressionist and Post-Impressionist masterpieces, which radically transformed the art world with their innovative techniques and depiction of light and color. Paintings by Claude Monet, Pierre-Auguste Renoir, and Edgar Degas transport us to idyllic landscapes, lively Parisian scenes, and captivating ballet performances.

Vincent van Gogh's mesmerizing self-portraits and Starry Night Over the Rhône exhibit his unique style and emotional depth, while Paul Cézanne's iconic still-life paintings redefine the genre.

The works of Post-Impressionist artists, such as Paul Gauguin and Henri de Toulouse-Lautrec, add a new dimension to the collection, with their vibrant colors and bold subject matters.

Picasso, Rodin, and More: Art at Its Finest

Beyond the Louvre and Musée d'Orsay, Paris offers an array of other art museums and galleries, each housing their own collection of artistic gems.

Musée Picasso

The Musée Picasso, located in the Marais district, celebrates the life and work of one of the most influential artists of the 20th century, Pablo Picasso. With over 5,000 works, including paintings, drawings, sculptures, and ceramics, the museum provides a comprehensive journey through the various periods of Picasso's artistic evolution.

Musée Rodin

For sculpture enthusiasts, the Musée Rodin is an absolute must-visit. The works of Auguste Rodin, one of the greatest sculptors of all time, are displayed in this museum, which is housed in the Hôtel Biron. His iconic sculptures, such as The Thinker and The Kiss, exude a raw emotionality and are celebrated for their innovative approach to form and movement.

In addition to these prominent museums, Paris's artistic treasures extend to smaller, intimate galleries scattered throughout the city. With its avant-garde design, the Centre Pompidou is home to an impressive collection of modern and contemporary art. It is home to works by artists like Wassily Kandinsky, Marc Chagall, and René Magritte, pushing the boundaries of artistic expression.

Venturing into the vibrant neighborhoods of Montmartre and Le Marais, we encounter numerous art studios and galleries, where emerging artists present their unique perspectives on the world. These spaces offer an opportunity to engage with contemporary art and support the work of new talents.

Chapter 2
Teen-Friendly Itineraries: The Best Sightseeing and Money-Saving Tips

In this chapter, we will explore some of the must-see iconic landmarks in Paris that are perfect for teenagers. Additionally, we'll provide money-saving tips to ensure your trip is budget-friendly and enjoyable.

Sightseeing Musts: Don't Miss These Iconic Landmarks

1. Notre-Dame Cathedral: A Gothic Marvel

The Notre-Dame Cathedral is one of the most renowned and revered landmarks in Paris. Its stunning Gothic architecture, intricate stone carvings, and majestic rose windows make it a must-visit attraction for art and history enthusiasts alike. The cathedral's history dates back over 850 years, and its construction showcases the architectural brilliance of the medieval period.

Visitors can marvel at the exterior facade, adorned with fascinating statues and gargoyles, and step inside to experience the grandeur of its interior. The soft glow of the stained glass windows creates a mesmerizing ambiance, encouraging visitors to reflect on the spiritual significance of this historic monument.

For those seeking an adventurous experience, consider climbing to the top of Notre-Dame. The ascent offers a unique vantage point of the city, providing breathtaking views of Paris's rooftops, the Seine River, and iconic landmarks like the Eiffel Tower and Sacré-Cœur Basilica. The opportunity to stand amidst the gargoyles and chimera adds a thrilling element to this memorable visit.

2. Eiffel Tower: Awe-Inspiring Views of the City

No trip to Paris is complete without visiting the Eiffel Tower, an enduring symbol of the city's grandeur and romance. This iconic iron lattice structure stands tall at

324 meters (1,063 feet) and offers stunning panoramic views of Paris from its three observation levels.

As you ascend the tower, the cityscape unfolds before your eyes, revealing the beauty of Paris's architecture, landmarks, and the meandering Seine River. From the Trocadéro Gardens to the distant Montmartre, each neighborhood showcases its unique charm from above.

The Eiffel Tower is equally captivating at night, when it sparkles with thousands of lights, putting on a dazzling light show that lasts for about ten minutes every hour. For a budget-friendly experience, head to the Champs de Mars, the park located at the foot of the tower, where you can lay out a blanket and enjoy the enchanting display without any cost.

3. The Palace of Versailles: A Royal Retreat

Just a short trip from Paris, the Palace of Versailles is a mesmerizing royal residence that promises a journey back in time. This opulent palace was the seat of power for French royalty, including King Louis XIV, known as the "Sun King."

The palace's interiors are a testament to luxury and grandeur, with lavishly decorated rooms like the Hall of Mirrors, adorned with glittering chandeliers and ornate gold trim. As you wander through the palace, you'll gain insights into the courtly life of the kings and queens of France.

The vast gardens of Versailles are an attraction in their own right, sprawling across 800 hectares (nearly 2,000 acres). The meticulously manicured lawns, magnificent fountains, and sculptures offer a fairytale-like setting for a leisurely stroll or a picnic with friends. On weekends, the gardens come alive with musical fountain shows, adding an extra touch of enchantment to your visit.

Sightseeing and Money-Saving Tips

- Paris Museum Pass: If you plan to visit multiple museums and monuments in Paris, consider purchasing a Paris Museum Pass. This pass provides access to over 50 attractions and can save you both time and money. You can choose from a variety of pass durations to fit your itinerary.

- Free Admission Days: Many museums in Paris offer free admission to visitors under 18 years old. Some museums also have free entry on the first Sunday of each month. Check the websites of the museums you wish to visit for specific information on free admission days.

- Explore by Foot or Bike: Paris is a highly walkable city, and exploring on foot allows you to discover hidden gems and charming neighborhoods that may not be easily accessible by other means of transportation. Renting a bike is another excellent option for navigating the city's streets, especially along the Seine River, which has dedicated bike paths.

- Pack a Picnic: Dining out in Paris can be delightful but also expensive. To enjoy a budget-friendly meal, consider packing a picnic and enjoying it in one of the city's beautiful parks or gardens. Paris has numerous outdoor spaces, such as Luxembourg Gardens and Parc des Buttes-Chaumont, where you can relax and savor your meal while taking in the picturesque surroundings.

- Student Discounts: Many attractions, including museums and theaters, offer student discounts with a valid student ID. Don't forget to check if the places you plan to visit have any special offers for students.

- Cultural Events and Festivals: Keep an eye out for free cultural events and festivals happening around the city. Paris hosts a variety of outdoor concerts, film screenings, and cultural festivities that are often free to attend. These events provide a unique opportunity to immerse yourself in the vibrant cultural scene of the city without spending a fortune.

By incorporating these sightseeing musts and money-savingtips into your Paris itinerary, you can make the most of your trip while staying within your budget. Now, let's delve deeper into additional money-saving tips and alternative attractions that will enhance your teen-friendly Paris adventure.

4. Explore Off-the-Beaten-Path Neighborhoods

While Paris's iconic landmarks are a must-see, don't overlook the charm of the city's lesser-known neighborhoods. Exploring off-the-beaten-path areas like Le Marais, Canal Saint-Martin, and Montmartre offers a more authentic and budget-friendly experience. These neighborhoods boast vibrant street art, quirky boutiques, and cozy cafes that are perfect for snapping Instagram-worthy photos and immersing yourself in the local culture.

5. Take Advantage of Free Walking Tours

Free walking tours are a fantastic way to discover Paris from a local's perspective without spending a dime upfront. These tours, led by passionate guides, allow you to explore the city's history, architecture, and hidden gems while providing valuable insights and recommendations for the rest of your trip. Keep in mind that while the tours are free, it's customary to tip the guide at the end of the tour if you enjoyed the experience.

6. Enjoy Budget-Friendly Eateries

Paris is a culinary haven, and experiencing French cuisine is undoubtedly a highlight of any trip. However, dining in restaurants can quickly add up, especially for budget-conscious travelers. To savor the city's delicious fare without breaking the bank, consider trying out local boulangeries (bakeries) and patisseries (pastry shops).

You can indulge in freshly baked croissants, baguettes, and delightful pastries at a fraction of the cost of a sit-down meal.

7. Participate in Free Events and Activities

Paris hosts an array of free events and activities throughout the year, offering entertainment and cultural experiences without the need to spend money. Check out the city's event calendars to find free concerts, open-air movie screenings, art exhibitions, and street performances that suit your interests.

8. Plan a Picnic by the Seine

One of the most budget-friendly and enjoyable ways to experience Paris like a local is to have a picnic by the Seine River. Purchase fresh produce from local markets, such as cheeses, fruits, and charcuterie, and find a cozy spot along the riverbank. Watching the boats pass by as you savor your picnic is a quintessential Parisian experience that won't dent your wallet.

9. Visit Public Parks and Gardens

Paris boasts a variety of public parks and gardens that offer tranquil oases amid the bustling city. Spend a leisurely afternoon in Luxembourg Gardens, Jardin des Tuileries, or Parc des Buttes-Chaumont, where you can stroll among lush greenery, lounge by fountains, and simply enjoy the beauty of nature without spending a cent.

10. Utilize Public Transportation

Navigating Paris is easy and cost-effective with its efficient public transportation system. The metro and buses can take you to most of the city's attractions and neighborhoods. Consider purchasing a Navigo Découverte pass, which provides unlimited travel within specific zones for a week, saving you money on individual tickets.

11. Explore Free Museums and Galleries

Paris is home to several museums and galleries that offer free admission year-round. The Petit Palais, Musée d'Art Moderne de la Ville de Paris, and Maison de la Photographie are just a few examples of places where you can admire art and exhibitions without spending a euro.

12. Discover Street Art in Belleville

Belleville is a vibrant neighborhood known for its thriving street art scene. Stroll through its colorful streets to discover impressive murals and urban art created by local and international artists. Exploring Belleville's street art is not only a budget-friendly activity but also a great way to experience contemporary art in an unconventional setting.

2.2

Insider Tips: How to Save Time and Money while Exploring Paris

As a teen adventurer in Paris, it's essential to make the most of your trip while being mindful of your budget. In this chapter, we will provide you with valuable insider tips to help you save time and money while exploring the city's popular tourist spots, as well as practical advice on enjoying budget-friendly dining and activities.

Avoiding Crowds at Popular Tourist Spots

Paris is a city that attracts millions of visitors every year, and while iconic landmarks and attractions are undoubtedly worth seeing, dealing with large crowds can be overwhelming and time-consuming. Here are some tips to help you make the most of your visit without getting caught in the hustle and bustle:

1. Early Morning Visits: Arrive at popular tourist spots as early as possible, preferably when they open. Many tourists tend to visit these attractions later in the day, so arriving early will give you a chance to explore without the crowds.

2. Book Tickets in Advance: For attractions that offer online ticketing, consider booking your tickets in advance. This not only saves time but may also offer skip-the-line privileges, allowing you to bypass long queues.

3. Plan Your Visit on Weekdays: Tourist attractions are generally less crowded on weekdays than on weekends, especially during the peak tourist season. If possible, schedule your visits on weekdays to avoid larger crowds.

4. Explore Lesser-Known Gems: While famous landmarks are must-see attractions, don't overlook the lesser-known gems scattered throughout the city. Exploring off-the-beaten-path sites not only offers a more intimate experience but also provides a respite from the tourist crowds.

5. Take Advantage of Evening Hours: Some museums and attractions, such as the Louvre and Musée d'Orsay, offer extended evening hours on specific days. These quieter hours are an excellent opportunity to enjoy the exhibits with fewer people around.

Budget-Friendly Dining and Activities

Paris is renowned for its culinary delights, but dining out can quickly add up, especially for a budget-conscious traveler. However, there are plenty of ways to savor delicious food and experience the city's culture without breaking the bank:

1. Street Food and Market Eats: Parisian street food offers a delicious and affordable way to taste local flavors. Head to a street market or a food truck for delectable crepes, falafels, and other portable treats that won't strain your wallet.

2. Picnics in the Parks: One of the best ways to enjoy Parisian cuisine on a budget is to have a picnic in one of the city's picturesque parks. Visit local bakeries and markets to pick up fresh baguettes, cheeses, and fruits for a delightful picnic experience.

3. Lunch Menus: Many restaurants offer prix-fixe lunch menus at a lower cost than their dinner menus. Take advantage of these lunch specials to enjoy a more affordable dining experience while still savoring gourmet dishes.

4. Seek Out Local Bistros and Cafés: Opt for quaint local bistros and cafés rather than touristy restaurants. Not only will you find more authentic cuisine, but you'll also likely pay lower prices.

5. Happy Hour Deals: If you're of legal drinking age, consider exploring the city's happy hour deals at bars and cafés. Enjoy discounted drinks and snacks during designated hours, often in the late afternoon or early evening.

6. Free and Low-Cost Activities: Paris offers a plethora of free or low-cost activities that allow you to experience the city's culture without spending a fortune. Some examples include attending free concerts, exploring art galleries with free admission, or participating in public events and festivals.

7. City Passes and Discount Cards: Investigate city passes or discount cards that offer combined access to attractions and public transportation. These passes can be a cost-effective way to explore multiple sights and save on transportation expenses.

8. Utilize Student Discounts: If you're a student, don't forget to inquire about student discounts at museums, attractions, and theaters. Many places offer reduced rates with a valid student ID.

9. Free Walking Tours: Joining a free walking tour is not only an excellent way to explore the city but also an opportunity to learn about Paris's history and culture from a knowledgeable local guide without any upfront cost. Don't forget to tip the guide if you enjoyed the experience.

10. Enjoy Free Outdoor Activities: Paris offers a myriad of free outdoor activities that can be both fun and budget-friendly. Stroll along the Seine River, visit public parks and gardens, or relax in outdoor squares while people-watching and soaking in the city's ambiance.

By following these insider tips on avoiding crowds at popular tourist spots and enjoying budget-friendly dining and activities, you can make the most of your time in Paris without overspending. Paris has something to offer for every traveler, and with a little bit of planning and savvy decision-making, you'll create cherished memories without sacrificing your budget.

Chapter 3
The Main Attractions and Hidden Gems of Paris

As a teen adventurer in Paris, you'll have the opportunity to explore not only the city's iconic main attractions but also its hidden gems that are often overlooked by tourists. In this chapter, we'll unveil some of these hidden treasures, taking you on a journey through the bohemian vibes of Montmartre, the historical significance of Père Lachaise Cemetery, and the picturesque urban oasis of Canal Saint-Martin.

Unveiling Paris's Hidden Gems

1. The Mystique of Montmartre: Art and Bohemian Vibes

Montmartre, located in the 18th arrondissement of Paris, is a neighborhood that exudes artistic flair, bohemian vibes, and a rich history. In the late 19th and early 20th centuries, Montmartre was a hub for artists, writers, and intellectuals, drawing inspiration from its charming streets and unique ambiance.

Sacré-Cœur Basilica: Our journey through Montmartre begins with the iconic Sacré-Cœur Basilica, perched on the highest point of the neighborhood. This stunning basilica, with its distinctive white domes, offers panoramic views of Paris, making it a favorite spot for both locals and visitors.

Place du Tertre: Just a stone's throw from Sacré-Cœur is the vibrant Place du Tertre. This bustling square is where artists gather to display their work and showcase their talents. Stroll through the square, observe artists at work, and perhaps get your portrait sketched as a one-of-a-kind souvenir.

Le Bateau-Lavoir: This historic building in Montmartre was once a meeting place for renowned artists like Pablo Picasso, Amedeo Modigliani, and Juan Gris. Today, it serves as an exhibition space and a reminder of Montmartre's bohemian past.

Moulin Rouge: While not entirely hidden, Moulin Rouge is an iconic cabaret that still captivates audiences with its lively performances. Although attending a show can be pricey, you can still soak in the atmosphere by snapping photos of the famous red windmill and the bohemian façade.

2. Père Lachaise Cemetery: A Walk through History

Père Lachaise Cemetery is not your typical tourist attraction, but it holds immense historical and cultural significance. Founded in 1804, it is one of the most visited cemeteries in the world and serves as the final resting place of numerous notable figures.

Tomb of Jim Morrison: The grave of legendary musician Jim Morrison, lead singer of The Doors, is among the most visited in the cemetery. Fans from around the world pay tribute to the rock icon by leaving flowers, notes, and memorabilia.

Oscar Wilde's Memorial: The Irish playwright and poet Oscar Wilde's tomb is an elaborate monument featuring a sculpture of a flying angel. It has become a symbol of artistic reverence and is often adorned with lipstick marks left by admirers.

Division 97: This section of the cemetery houses the Communards' Wall, where the remains of individuals involved in the Paris Commune of 1871 are interred. The wall stands as a memorial to those who fought for social justice and workers' rights during that tumultuous period.

Walking Among History: As you wander through Père Lachaise, you'll encounter the graves of renowned artists, writers, politicians, and other historical figures, including Frédéric Chopin, Edith Piaf, Marcel Proust, and Édouard Manet, to name just a few. It's a fascinating journey through time and a unique opportunity to pay homage to some of history's greatest minds.

3. Canal Saint-Martin: A Picturesque Urban Oasis

Away from the bustling tourist hotspots, Canal Saint-Martin offers a serene and picturesque escape in the heart of the city. This 4.5-kilometer-long waterway, lined with trees and footbridges, is a favorite spot for Parisians seeking a peaceful retreat.

Canal Walks: Take a leisurely stroll along the canal's banks, where you can enjoy the tranquility of the water and the surrounding greenery. The tree-lined pathways offer a shaded respite, especially on sunny days.

Picnic by the Canal: Join the locals in one of their favorite pastimes: picnicking by the water. Grab some delicious treats from local bakeries or food markets, spread out a blanket, and enjoy a delightful picnic with friends while watching boats pass by.

Evening Gatherings: In the evenings, the canal comes alive with gatherings of friends and families, enjoying each other's company along the water's edge. Join the friendly atmosphere, and perhaps strike up a conversation with the locals. It's a fantastic way to experience the true essence of Parisian life.

Canal Bridges: The canal is dotted with charming footbridges that add to its picturesque appeal. One of the most famous is the Pont des Arts, known for its once-covered padlocks symbolizing eternal love. While the padlocks have been removed, the bridge remains a popular spot for couples to take romantic walks.

3.2

Explore the Iconic Landmarks Every Teen Should See

In this chapter, we will embark on a journey through some of the most iconic landmarks in Paris that every teen adventurer should experience. These awe-inspiring attractions hold historical significance, architectural splendor, and cultural importance, making them an essential part of any Parisian itinerary.

Explore the Iconic Landmarks Every Teen Should See

1. The Majestic Arc de Triomphe and Champs-Élysées

French pride is symbolized by the Arc de Triomphe.
Standing proudly at the western end of the Champs-
Élysées, the Arc de Triomphe is an iconic symbol of
French national pride and a monument of grandeur.
Commissioned by Napoleon Bonaparte in 1806, the
arch commemorates the victories of the French army
and honors those who fought and died for France.

As you approach the Arc de Triomphe, you'll be greeted by its impressive size and intricate sculptures. The arch's colossal reliefs depict scenes of French military triumphs and patriotic allegories. For a breathtaking panoramic view of Paris, climb to the top of the monument, where you can witness the convergence of twelve grand avenues radiating from the arch's center, including the famous Champs-Élysées.

Champs-Élysées: The Grand Avenue of Elegance and Glamour
From the Arc de Triomphe, the Champs-Élysées stretches like a graceful ribbon, leading you through a glamorous avenue filled with high-end boutiques, luxurious hotels, and chic cafés. Often called "the most beautiful avenue in the world," the Champs-Élysées is a magnet for shoppers, fashion enthusiasts, and culture seekers.

Stroll down this elegant boulevard to admire its Parisian charm and sophisticated ambiance. Stop by renowned shops like Louis Vuitton and Cartier or visit the flagship stores of popular French brands. If you're a car enthusiast, don't miss the flagship showrooms of luxury car manufacturers, where you can marvel at the latest models.

2. The Magnificent Opéra Garnier and Les Invalides

Opéra Garnier: A Palatial Opera House

Opéra Garnier, also known as Palais Garnier, is a splendid opera house that boasts opulent architecture and a rich artistic legacy. Designed by Charles Garnier and completed in 1875, this magnificent building exudes the grandeur of the Second Empire, with its ornate façade and majestic interiors.

A guided tour of Opéra Garnier allows you to explore the auditorium's lavish décor, including the mesmerizing ceiling painted by Marc Chagall. The sumptuous Grand Foyer, adorned with crystal chandeliers and gilded accents, will transport you back to the belle époque era, when Paris was a thriving cultural capital.

Les Invalides: A Monument to French Military History

Les Invalides, officially known as Hôtel des Invalides, is a historic complex that honors France's military history and houses the tomb of one of the country's most renowned leaders, Napoleon Bonaparte. Originally constructed as a veterans' retirement home by Louis XIV, the complex later became a military museum and a place of national significance.

Inside Les Invalides, you'll find the Musée de l'Armée (Army Museum), which showcases an extensive collection of military artifacts, weapons, and uniforms from different periods of French history. One of the highlights of the museum is the monumental Dome Church, where Napoleon's tomb lies beneath a magnificent golden dome.

3. The Breathtaking Sacré-Cœur Basilica

Montmartre's Crown Jewel
Perched atop the hill of Montmartre, the Sacré-Cœur Basilica is an ethereal landmark that offers a spiritual retreat and breathtaking views of Paris. Constructed in the late 19th and early 20th centuries as a symbol of national reconciliation following the Franco-Prussian War, the basilica's stunning white exterior and Romano-Byzantine architecture make it an enchanting sight.

Inside the Sacré-Cœur, the grandiose interior features intricate mosaics that narrate religious stories and scenes. Visitors are invited to find moments of reflection and solace while enjoying the tranquil ambiance.

The panoramic terrace surrounding the basilica provides an unparalleled vista of Paris. From here, you can admire the city's iconic landmarks, such as the Eiffel Tower, the Arc de Triomphe, and Notre-Dame Cathedral. Sunset is an ideal time to visit, as the warm hues of the setting sun bathe the city in a golden glow, creating a magical experience.

Chapter 4
Embracing Local Culture and Cuisine

Paris is not only a city of iconic landmarks and historical treasures but also a hub of vibrant local culture and delectable cuisine. In this chapter, we will explore the best tips for avoiding crowds in Paris, uncovering offbeat places and activities that provide a more intimate experience. Additionally, we will delve into the local hangouts loved by Parisian teens, allowing you to immerse yourself in the city's authentic and youthful ambiance.

Best Tips for Avoiding Crowds in Paris

Paris, being one of the most popular tourist destinations in the world, can get crowded, especially during peak seasons. To make the most of your visit without feeling overwhelmed by tourist throngs, consider these tips for exploring the city off the beaten path:

1. Early Morning Strolls: Start your day early with a tranquil walk along the Seine River or through charming neighborhoods like Le Marais. The city is remarkably peaceful in the early hours, giving you a chance to appreciate its beauty without the crowds.

2. Discover Offbeat Districts: While the major attractions are undoubtedly must-see, don't limit your exploration to only the well-known areas. Paris is a city of diverse neighborhoods, each offering a unique atmosphere. Venture into places like Belleville, Canal Saint-Martin, or Butte-aux-Cailles to experience the city's authentic charm.

3. Seine River Cruise at Sunset: Skip the daytime crowds and opt for a Seine River cruise during sunset. This magical experience allows you to witness iconic landmarks illuminated against the darkening sky, creating a captivating and romantic ambiance.

4. Visit Lesser-Known Museums: While the Louvre and Musée d'Orsay are exceptional museums, consider visiting lesser-known art galleries and museums that offer equally fascinating collections. The Musée de la Chasse et de la Nature or the Musée de Montmartre are great examples of offbeat venues.

5. Explore Parks and Gardens: Seek refuge in the city's beautiful parks and gardens. Jardin des Plantes, Parc des Buttes-Chaumont, and Parc Monceau are serene oases where you can enjoy a leisurely stroll or a relaxing picnic away from the bustling crowds.

6. Take the Road Less Traveled: Wander through hidden passages and alleys known as "passages couverts" that offer a glimpse into Paris's charming past. These covered passages house unique shops, restaurants, and galleries, perfect for a peaceful escape from the city's busiest streets.

4.2

Local Hangouts Loved by Parisian Teens

To truly embrace the local culture and experience Paris like a true Parisian teen, immerse yourself in the city's favored hangouts and activities:

1. Cafés and Patisseries: Parisians have a deep appreciation for coffee and pastries. Spend leisurely afternoons at cozy cafés like Café de Flore or Les Deux Magots in Saint-Germain-des-Prés, where you can enjoy a "café au lait" and indulge in a delectable "croissant" or "pain au chocolat."

2. Flea Markets and Vintage Shopping: Hunt for unique finds at the city's lively flea markets. Marché aux Puces de Saint-Ouen is one of the largest and most famous, offering vintage clothing, antiques, and quirky treasures. You'll have a blast exploring these markets with fellow fashion enthusiasts.

3. Hangout Spots by the Seine: Join Parisian teens who gather by the Seine River to relax, chat, and enjoy picnics together. The quays along the riverbanks become impromptu gathering spots, especially during warm evenings.

4. Skate Parks and Urban Art: For teens interested in urban culture, Paris offers various skate parks and street art spots. Head to La Place de la République, where you can witness both impressive tricks by skaters and vibrant street murals.

5. Music and Street Performances: Keep an eye out for street performers, especially in popular areas like Montmartre and the Latin Quarter. Talented musicians, dancers, and magicians add a touch of charm to Parisian streets, making your visit even more delightful.

6. Outdoor Cinema and Open-Air Concerts: During the summer months, Paris hosts outdoor cinema screenings and open-air concerts in parks and squares. These events attract a young and lively crowd, offering a fantastic opportunity to experience Parisian culture under the stars.

7. Local Festivals and Fairs: Check out local festivals and fairs happening during your visit. Whether it's a neighborhood celebration or a food festival, these events provide insight into the city's vibrant community life.

8. Picnics in the Parks: Joining friends for a picnic in one of Paris's beautiful parks is a favorite pastime for local teens. Grab some delicious treats from a nearby bakery or market, find a spot on the grass, and enjoy a leisurely meal together.

Dining like a Parisian: Must-Try French Food and Drinks

Paris is a city that delights the senses, and its culinary scene is no exception. In this chapter, we will delve deeper into the world of French gastronomy, exploring the must-try French food and drinks that are beloved by Parisians and visitors alike. From delightful pastries and savory treats to the art of savoring coffee, wine, and more, this gastronomic journey will leave you with a true taste of Paris.

Delectable Pastries and Treats

French pastries are an integral part of the country's culinary heritage, and Paris boasts some of the finest patisseries in the world. Satisfy your sweet tooth with these delightful treats:

1. Croissant: A Parisian Breakfast Staple

The croissant is a breakfast essential in Paris, and biting into a buttery and flaky croissant is an experience you won't forget. Whether you choose the classic version or indulge in a filled croissant with chocolate, almond cream, or fruit preserves, each bite is a taste of pure bliss. Pair it with a café au lait or hot chocolate for a truly authentic Parisian breakfast.

2. Pain au Chocolat: Chocolate-Filled Bliss

Similar to the croissant, the pain au chocolat is another breakfast favorite. Filled with rich and gooey chocolate, each bite is a moment of sheer indulgence. Enjoy it as a mid-morning or afternoon snack with a cup of coffee.

3. Macarons: Colorful Confections

Macarons are delicate almond-based cookies filled with flavored ganache, buttercream, or fruit preserves. Paris is renowned for its colorful macarons, and the city's patisseries offer an array of flavors, from traditional ones like raspberry and pistachio to more unique combinations like salted caramel and lavender. Savor these sweet treats as a delightful souvenir to take home.

4. Éclairs: Cream-Filled Goodness

Éclairs are a staple in French patisseries, and each one is a work of art. These long choux pastry shells are filled with flavored cream and topped with glossy icing. From classic vanilla to rich chocolate or coffee, the choice is yours. Don't be shocked if you end up returning for more.

5. Tarte Tatin: A Caramelized Delight

Originating from the Loir-et-Cher region, tarte Tatin is an upside-down caramelized apple tart. The combination of tender apples and caramelized sugar creates a heavenly contrast of flavors. Served warm with a scoop of vanilla ice cream, this rustic dessert is a true French classic.

Savory Delights: From Croissants to Crêpes

French cuisine extends beyond pastries to savory delights that will satisfy your appetite and introduce you to the diverse flavors of Paris:

1. Croque-Monsieur: A Gourmet Grilled Sandwich

A croque-monsieur is a quintessential French bistro dish that elevates the humble grilled cheese sandwich to a gourmet delight. Made with ham, creamy béchamel sauce, and grated cheese, it's then toasted to perfection. For an extra touch of indulgence, try the croque-madame, which is topped with a fried egg.

2. Quiche Lorraine: A Savory Pie

Quiche Lorraine is a savory pie originating from the Lorraine region. Filled with a rich mixture of eggs, cream, cheese, and bacon or ham, it's a hearty and flavorful dish. The buttery pastry crust complements the creamy filling, making it a delightful choice for a light lunch or dinner.

3. Coq au Vin: A Hearty French Stew

Coq au vin is a traditional French dish that showcases the art of slow-cooking. It features chicken braised in red wine, along with mushrooms, onions, and bacon. The slow cooking process infuses the chicken with the flavors of the wine and aromatics, resulting in a tender and flavorful stew.

4. Ratatouille: A Mediterranean Delight
Ratatouille is a vibrant vegetable stew made with tomatoes, eggplants, zucchinis, bell peppers, and onions, seasoned with fragrant herbs like thyme and basil. It's a vegetarian delight that bursts with the flavors of the Mediterranean. Served with crusty bread or as a side to meat dishes, it's a comforting and healthy choice.

5. Crêpes: Versatile Thin Pancakes

Crêpes are thin pancakes that can be enjoyed sweet or savory, making them a versatile treat. The classic sweet version is often served with Nutella, jam, or sugar, while savory options may include ham, cheese, and mushrooms. Whether enjoyed as a quick street snack or a sit-down meal, crêpes are a favorite for locals and tourists alike.

Sip like a Parisian: Coffee, Wine, and More

Parisian culture revolves around savoring beverages with a sense of leisure and appreciation. Join the locals in their love for these iconic drinks:

1. Café Culture: Savoring Coffee
Coffee is a daily ritual for Parisians, and the café culture is deeply ingrained in the city's lifestyle. Order a classic "café" for a small cup of espresso or try "café crème" for a coffee with milk. Take your time, relax at a café terrace, and people-watch while you enjoy your coffee.

2. Wine: A Celebration of Terroir
France is renowned for its exceptional wine, and Paris offers a diverse selection from various regions. Indulge in a glass of Bordeaux, Burgundy, or Champagne with your meals, as wine is an integral part of French dining. Visit a local wine bar or participate in a wine tasting to deepen your appreciation of this centuries-old tradition.

3. Apéritif: Pre-Dinner Delights
Before dinner, Parisians often enjoy an apéritif, a pre-meal drink that stimulates the appetite. Traditional choices include "Kir" (white wine with crème de cassis), "Pastis" (an anise-flavored spirit), or "Lillet" (a wine-based aperitif). Sip on these drinks at a neighborhood bistro or a trendy rooftop bar.

4. Hot Chocolate: A Treat for Chocoholics
Parisian hot chocolate, or "chocolat chaud," is a luxurious and velvety treat. Made with melted chocolate

and steamed milk, it's a warm and comforting beverage, especially during the colder months. Visit a renowned chocolaterie like Angelina or Jacques Genin to experience this delectable drink at its finest.

5. Evian and Tap Water: A Difference in Cost
When dining in Paris, it's essential to know that tap water is safe to drink and is generally offered for free at restaurants. However, if you prefer bottled water, be aware that it can be quite expensive in restaurants. To save on costs, consider ordering "une carafe d'eau" (a carafe of tap water) instead of bottled water.

Savoring French Cuisine: A Gastronomic Experience

French cuisine is not just about the individual dishes; it's about the entire dining experience. Parisians take their time to savor each meal and appreciate the flavors, textures, and aromas that come together to create a memorable dining experience. When indulging in French cuisine, keep the following tips in mind:

1. Relish the Art of Slow Dining
In Paris, meals are more than just a way to refuel; they are a social event to enjoy with family and friends. Embrace the art of slow dining and take your time to enjoy each course. Engage in conversation, savor the flavors, and let the experience unfold at a leisurely pace.

2. Respect Local Dining Customs

When dining out, respect local customs and etiquette. For example, it's common practice to greet restaurant staff with a polite "Bonjour" upon entering, and a "Merci, au revoir" when leaving. Additionally, it's customary to wait for your host or hostess to say "Bon appétit" before you begin your meal.

3. Seasonal and Local Ingredients
French cuisine celebrates seasonal and locally sourced ingredients, which is evident in the ever-changing menu offerings. Indulge in dishes that showcase the flavors of the season, and savor the freshness of ingredients carefully selected by talented chefs.

4. Try the Daily Specials
Many Parisian restaurants offer daily specials or "plat du jour," which are dishes prepared with the freshest ingredients available that day. Trying the daily specials gives you a chance to taste unique creations crafted by the chef.

5. The Joy of Fromage (Cheese)
France is famous for its incredible variety of cheeses, and Parisian menus often feature a selection of fromage. Don't miss the opportunity to savor a cheese platter as a prelude or conclusion to your meal. Pair the cheeses with a glass of wine for a delightful taste experience.

Exploring Food Markets and Food Halls

To truly immerse yourself in Parisian gastronomy, explore the city's vibrant food markets and food halls. Some must-visit places include:

1. Marché des Enfants Rouges: A Historic Covered Market

Located in the trendy Marais district, Marché des Enfants Rouges is the oldest covered market in Paris. Here, you can sample a variety of cuisines, from French classics to international delights, and even grab a seat at one of the market's charming eateries.

2. Marché Bastille: A Parisian Favorite

Marché Bastille is a bustling market known for its fresh produce, cheeses, meats, and artisanal products. Join the locals as they shop for ingredients to create their favorite dishes or simply wander through the market and take in the vibrant atmosphere.

3. La Grande Épicerie de Paris: Food Hall Extravaganza

Situated in the elegant Le Bon Marché department store, La Grande Épicerie de Paris is a paradise for food enthusiasts. Explore the aisles filled with gourmet delights, from fresh seafood and cheeses to artisan chocolates and pastries. The food hall offers a delightful selection of ready-to-eat items, making it a perfect spot for a gourmet picnic.

4. Experience the Outdoor Markets

If you happen to visit Paris on specific days, you can enjoy the charm of outdoor markets in different neighborhoods. From the flower markets on Île de la Cité to the vintage markets in Le Marais, each market offers its own unique appeal and an opportunity to immerse yourself in the local culture.

4.3

Nightlife for Teens: Clubs, Entertainment, and Fun

When the sun sets in Paris, the city comes alive with a vibrant nightlife that offers a mix of entertainment, music, and fun. In this chapter, we will explore the nightlife options that cater to teens, ensuring an unforgettable experience in the City of Lights. From teen-friendly clubs and venues to unique entertainment experiences, Paris has something exciting to offer for every young adventurer.

1.Teen-Friendly Clubs and Venues

While Paris is known for its sophisticated nightlife, there are plenty of venues that are welcoming to teenagers and offer a safe and enjoyable atmosphere. Here are some of the best teen-friendly clubs and places to experience the city's nightlife:

Le Trabendo
Le Trabendo, located in the Parc de la Villette, is one of the city's most popular concert venues for teens. The club regularly hosts all-ages concerts and events, featuring a diverse lineup of local and international artists across various genres. Whether you're into rock, pop, hip-hop, or electronic music, Le Trabendo promises an exciting night of live performances. Keep an eye out for special themed nights or concerts featuring emerging artists, as these events offer a unique and authentic experience.

Wanderlust
Situated on the banks of the Seine River, Wanderlust is a trendy and youthful hotspot. During the day, it serves as a restaurant and bar with a terrace overlooking the river. However, at night, it transforms into a buzzing club with DJs spinning energetic beats. Wanderlust occasionally hosts teen-focused events or themed parties, making it an excellent destination for young music enthusiasts. Check their schedule for events like silent discos, retro-themed nights, or guest DJ performances.

L'International
L'International is a lively music venue in the hip Oberkampf neighborhood, known for its vibrant nightlife

scene. The club features regular concerts and DJ sets, showcasing up-and-coming artists and established acts. The atmosphere is relaxed, making it an ideal spot for teens to enjoy live music and make new friends. Check their calendar for "open mic" nights or showcases of local bands, as these events provide an opportunity to discover fresh talent.

Le Petit Bain
Le Petit Bain is a unique cultural center and concert venue situated on a floating barge on the Seine River. The venue hosts a diverse range of events, including concerts, workshops, and themed parties. With a panoramic view of the river and the city skyline, Le Petit Bain offers a memorable and Instagram-worthy experience for teens. Keep an eye out for themed parties, electro-pop nights, or indie band performances, as these events cater to a young and energetic crowd.

La Bellevilloise
La Bellevilloise is a multifunctional space that combines a bar, concert hall, and nightclub. It's a popular spot for young locals, and its eclectic programming ensures there's always something exciting happening. From live music and DJ nights to poetry slams and art exhibitions, La Bellevilloise offers a diverse and dynamic nightlife experience. Check their website for themed parties, "80s vs. 90s" dance nights, or acoustic showcases, as these events attract a young and diverse audience.

2. Unique Entertainment Experiences

Beyond traditional clubs, Paris offers a range of unique and entertaining experiences that teens will love. Here are some alternative nightlife options to consider:

Rooftop Bars and Terraces

Enjoy breathtaking views of the city's iconic landmarks from one of Paris's rooftop bars and terraces. Some venues offer special events and theme nights that cater to younger crowds. Whether it's dancing under the stars or sipping mocktails with friends, rooftop bars provide a memorable and sophisticated experience. Check out venues like Perchoir Marais, Le Jardin Suspendu, or Mama Shelter for their youthful and trendy rooftop events.

Outdoor Cinema

During the warmer months, Paris comes alive with outdoor cinema screenings in parks and public spaces. Gather with friends and locals to watch classic films or recent blockbusters under the starry sky. Pack a picnic and enjoy a cinematic experience like no other. Keep an eye out for "cinéma en plein air" events at Parc de la Villette, Parc de la Butte-du-Chapeau-Rouge, or Parc de la Villette.

Nighttime Boat Cruises

Explore the Seine River in a different light with nighttime boat cruises. Several operators offer boat tours with live music, dinner, and dancing on board. Glide past illuminated landmarks like the Eiffel Tower, Notre-Dame Cathedral, and the Louvre, creating magical memories that will last a lifetime. Some boat cruises offer special teen-oriented nights with themed parties or international music.

Escape Games and Laser Tag
For an adrenaline-filled and interactive night out, consider participating in an escape game or a game of laser tag. These activities are popular among teens, as they require teamwork, problem-solving skills, and a sense of adventure. Paris has several venues offering these thrilling experiences that will keep you on the edge of your seat. Check out locations like "Prizoners," "HintHunt," or "Laser Game Evolution" for unforgettable adventures.

Night Markets
Certain neighborhoods in Paris host night markets, where you can browse stalls selling unique crafts, vintage clothing, and artisanal goods. These markets often feature live music, street performances, and food trucks, creating a lively and festive atmosphere. Keep an eye out for "Marché de la Création" in the Marais or "Marché Bastille" for a youthful and artistic night market experience.

3. Safety and Etiquette Tips

As with any nightlife experience, it's essential to prioritize safety and adhere to local etiquette. Here are some tips to ensure a safe and enjoyable night out in Paris:

Stick Together

If you're out with a group of friends, make a pact to stick together throughout the night. Establish a meeting point in case anyone gets separated, and look out for each other. Avoid isolated or poorly lit areas, and stay in well-populated and well-lit places.

Plan Your Transport

Before heading out, plan your transportation for the night. Familiarize yourself with the city's public transportation schedule and options for getting back to your accommodation safely. Always carry a fully charged phone or have a portable charger on hand.

Respect the Venue Rules

When visiting clubs or music venues, respect their rules and guidelines. Some places may have dress codes or age restrictions for certain events. Make sure to carry a valid ID if you plan on attendingcertain venues that require age verification.

Be Mindful of Personal Belongings

In crowded places, such as concerts or busy streets, be cautious of your personal belongings. Keep your wallet, phone, and other valuables locked away. Avoid carrying large amounts of cash and consider using a small crossbody bag or a secure backpack to keep your belongings close to you.

Stay Hydrated and Take Breaks

If you're dancing or participating in energetic activities, remember to stay hydrated. Some venues may provide water stations, but it's a good idea to bring a refillable water bottle with you. Take occasional breaks to rest and recharge, especially if you're attending an all-night event.

Alcohol and Substance Awareness

As a teen, you may be curious about trying new experiences, but it's essential to be cautious when it comes to alcohol and substances. In France, the legal drinking age is 18, and it's crucial to adhere to the law. If you're of legal age and choose to drink, do so responsibly and know your limits. Never accept drinks from strangers, and be aware of the contents of any beverages you consume.

4. Respect the Local Culture

Participating in the nightlife in Paris is a fantastic way to experience the city's vibrancy and energy, but it's also essential to respect the local culture and customs. Parisians take pride in their city, and showing respect for their traditions will make your experience more enjoyable:

Dress Code

Some clubs and venues may have a dress code, so it's a good idea to check the establishment's website or social media pages for guidelines. In general, Parisians have a stylish and sophisticated fashion sense, so dressing neatly and tastefully will help you blend in with the local crowd.

Language
While English is widely spoken in tourist areas, attempting to speak a few basic phrases in French can go a long way in showing respect for the local culture. Simple greetings like "Bonjour" (Hello), "Merci" (Thank you), and "Au revoir" (Goodbye) will be appreciated by the locals.

Tipping
Tipping is not obligatory in France, as a service charge is often included in the bill at restaurants and bars. However, leaving a small tip as a gesture of appreciation for excellent service is a common practice.

5. Socialize and Make Friends

The nightlife scene in Paris provides an excellent opportunity to meet new people and make friends from around the world. Don't be afraid to strike up conversations with other teens and locals, especially if you're attending social events or concerts. Engaging with others will enhance your experience and may lead to memorable encounters and new friendships.

6. Cultural Events and Festivals

Beyond the regular nightlife venues, Paris hosts various cultural events and festivals that can be enjoyed by teens. Check the city's event calendars for art exhibitions, live performances, film festivals, and street fairs. These events offer unique insights into the city's artistic and cultural heritage.

7. Safety Reminders

While exploring the Parisian nightlife, it's essential to prioritize your safety and well-being. Here are some general safety reminders:

Travel in Groups: Whenever possible, travel in a group, especially when exploring unfamiliar areas or late at night.

Keep to well-lit areas: Keep to well-lit roadways and stay away from dark or remote regions.

Keep Emergency Contacts: Make sure you have emergency contacts programmed in your phone and a physical copy of important phone numbers in case your phone runs out of battery.

Know Your Limits: If you choose to consume alcohol, do so responsibly and know your limits. Avoid accepting drinks from strangers.

Keep an eye on your surroundings: Pay attention to your surroundings and trust your instincts. If you feel uncomfortable or unsafe, leave the area and seek assistance.

Chapter 5
Maps, Accommodations, and
Transportation Tips

Paris is a sprawling and enchanting city with a rich history and numerous attractions waiting to be explored. In this chapter, we will delve into essential tips for navigating the city, understanding the Paris Metro system, and utilizing helpful maps and navigation apps to ensure a smooth and enjoyable trip. Additionally, we will explore various accommodation options suitable for teens, making your stay in Paris a memorable and comfortable one.

Navigating Paris with Maps and Transport

Paris Metro: An Efficient Way to Get Around
The Paris Metro is one of the most efficient and convenient methods of transportation in the city. With its extensive network of 16 lines, the metro connects various neighborhoods, attractions, and landmarks, making it easy for visitors to navigate the city. Here are all the following information you need to know about using the Paris Metro:

1. Ticket Types

Before hopping on the metro, you'll need to purchase a ticket. The Paris Metro operates on a zone system, with Zone 1 covering the central part of the city. The majority of tourism attractions are found in Zone 1. Tickets can be purchased at metro stations from ticket machines or ticket counters. For short stays, consider buying single-use tickets (t+ tickets) or packs of 10 tickets, known as "carnets," for discounted fares.

2. Navigating the Metro Map

The metro map can initially appear daunting with its intricate network of lines, but it's relatively easy to follow once you understand the color-coded lines and station names. The iconic Paris Metro map features intersecting lines, each representing a different metro line. When planning your route, determine your starting station and destination station, then follow the lines that connect the two. Transfers between lines are marked with white circles on the map.

3. Timings and Frequencies

The Paris Metro typically operates from around 5:30 AM until 12:30 AM, with slight variations depending on the line and station. Trains run frequently, especially during peak hours, making it convenient for tourists to explore the city at any time of day.

4. Metro Etiquette

While using the metro, it's essential to follow some common courtesy and etiquette guidelines. Let passengers exit the train before boarding, avoid blocking doors, and be mindful of your belongings. Keep in mind that the first car of each train is often reserved for women and children during certain hours.

Helpful Maps and Navigation Apps

In addition to the official Paris Metro map, several other resources can assist you in navigating the city:

1. Paris Street Maps

Obtaining a physical street map of Paris is a great way to get an overview of the city's layout and street names. Free city maps are available at many hotels, visitor information centers, and book stores. These maps can help you plan walking routes between attractions or find nearby restaurants and amenities.

2. Smartphone Navigation Apps

There are several navigation apps that can be immensely helpful during your time in Paris. Apps like Google Maps, Apple Maps, and Citymapper provide real-time navigation, public transportation schedules, and directions to your destination. With these apps, you can find the best metro routes, bus connections, and even get estimated travel times for walking.

3. Paris Metro Apps

For a more specialized approach to navigating the Paris Metro, consider downloading dedicated metro apps. Apps like RATP and Next Stop Paris offer interactive metro maps, real-time train schedules, and alerts about any service disruptions. They can help you plan your route efficiently and avoid any unnecessary delays.

4. Velib Bike Sharing App

Velib is Paris's popular bike-sharing system, allowing you to rent bikes from various stations across the city. The Velib app provides real-time information on bike availability, station locations, and rental options. Biking can be an enjoyable and eco-friendly way to explore Paris's neighborhoods and scenic routes.

5. City Guides

Many travel guidebooks and websites offer comprehensive city guides for Paris, including maps and recommendations for top attractions, restaurants, and hidden gems. These guides can serve as a valuable resource during your trip and help you plan your days more effectively.

6. Offline Maps

To avoid data roaming charges, consider downloading offline maps of Paris before your trip. Many navigation apps offer this feature, allowing you to access maps and directions without an internet connection. This is especially useful if you plan on exploring the city without access to Wi-Fi.

5.2

The Perfect Place to Stay: Hotels, Airbnb, and More

Finding the perfect place to stay in Paris is an essential part of planning your trip. The city offers a diverse range of accommodations, from luxury hotels to cozy farmhouses, catering to different preferences and budgets. In this chapter, we will explore teen-friendly accommodations in Paris and unique farmhouse stays near the city, providing you with extensive and detailed information to make the best choice for your stay.

Teen-Friendly Accommodations in Paris
When traveling as a teen, it's essential to find accommodations that cater to your needs and provide a comfortable and enjoyable experience. Luckily, Paris offers a wide selection of teen-friendly options:

Youth Hostels

Youth hostels are a popular choice for young travelers, offering budget-friendly rates and a sociable atmosphere. In Paris, many hostels provide dormitory-style rooms with bunk beds, creating a fun and communal environment for meeting fellow travelers. Some hostels also offer private rooms for small groups or families seeking a bit more privacy.

One of the benefits of staying in a hostel is the opportunity to participate in organized activities, such as city tours, pub crawls, and cultural events. These activities can be an excellent way to explore the city and make new friends from around the world.

Boutique Hotels

For teens seeking a more stylish and personalized experience, boutique hotels are an excellent option. Boutique hotels are smaller, independently-owned establishments that focus on providing unique and upscale accommodations. These hotels often have distinct decor and offer personalized services, creating a memorable and immersive experience.

Some boutique hotels in Paris cater specifically to families and teens, offering amenities like game rooms, rooftop terraces, and teen-focused activities. Staying in a boutique hotel allows you to enjoy the comforts of a luxury hotel while immersing yourself in Paris's local charm.

Apartment Rentals

Apartment rentals, such as those offered through Airbnb, provide a home-away-from-home experience for teens traveling with family or friends. Renting an apartment allows for more space and privacy, as well as the opportunity to cook meals and live like a local. This option is ideal for teens who prefer a more independent and flexible travel experience.

When booking an apartment rental, be sure to read reviews from previous guests and check the listing for amenities such as Wi-Fi, kitchen facilities, and proximity to public transportation.

Hostel-Hotels Hybrid

A newer trend in the hospitality industry, hostel-hotels hybrids, combines the social atmosphere of a hostel with the comforts of a hotel. These establishments offer private rooms, similar to a traditional hotel, but also feature shared spaces like communal kitchens, lounges, and game areas, akin to a hostel.

Hostel-hotel hybrids are a great option for teens who want the best of both worlds - the privacy of a hotel room and the opportunity to socialize and meet other travelers in shared common areas.

Unique Farmhouse Stays near Paris

If you're looking to escape the bustling city and immerse yourself in the picturesque countryside, consider booking a farmhouse stay near Paris. These charming accommodations offer a peaceful retreat while still providing easy access to the city. Here are some farmhouse stay options worth considering:

Charming Bed and Breakfasts

Charming bed and breakfasts nestled in the countryside offer a warm and welcoming ambiance. These quaint establishments are often run by locals who take pride in offering a personalized experience for their guests. Wake up to the sound of birds chirping, enjoy a delicious homemade breakfast, and breathe in the fresh country air.

Bed and breakfasts are a great option for teens looking for a relaxing and intimate getaway while still being within reach of Paris's attractions.

Rustic Farmhouses

For a more rustic experience, consider booking a stay at a traditional farmhouse. These rustic accommodations provide an authentic glimpse into rural French life, with features like exposed wooden beams, cozy fireplaces, and sprawling gardens.

Many farmhouses offer outdoor activities, such as biking, hiking, and picnicking, making them ideal for teens who enjoy outdoor adventures. It's a wonderful way to unwind after a day of sightseeing in the city.

Farm Stays with Animals

Some farmhouse stays offer the unique opportunity to interact with animals. These farm stays are perfect for animal-loving teens who want to experience life on a working farm. Spend your days feeding chickens, collecting fresh eggs, and meeting friendly farm animals.

Farm stays with animals are educational and fun, providing an enriching experience that will be remembered long after your trip.

Vineyard Retreats

If you have a passion for wine and vineyards, consider staying at a vineyard retreat near Paris. These serene accommodations are often surrounded by vineyards, providing a tranquil and picturesque setting.

Vineyard retreats offer wine tastings, guided tours, and the chance to learn about the winemaking process. It's a unique experience for teens interested in the world of viticulture and oenology.

How to Choose the Right Accommodation

It can be difficult to choose the best hotel with so many options available. Here are some things to think about before you decide:

Budget

Determine your budget before starting your search. Hostels and budget hotels offer the most affordable options, while boutique hotels and apartment rentals are generally more expensive. Farmhouse stays may vary in price depending on the amenities and location.

Location
Consider the location of your chosen accommodation in relation to the attractions and neighborhoods you plan to visit. Staying near a metro station or public transportation hub can make getting around the city more convenient.

Amenities and Services
Hostels often offer social activities and communal spaces, while hotels may provide amenities like room service, fitness centers, and on-site dining options. Farmhouse stays offer a unique set of amenities, such as outdoor activities and farm-to-table dining.

Reviews and Ratings
Reading reviews and ratings from previous guests can provide valuable insights into the quality and customer service of a particular accommodation. Look for properties with positive feedback from other travelers.

Safety and Security
Ensure that your chosen accommodation has appropriate safety measures in place. Hostels should have secure lockers for belongings, while hotels and rentals should have reliable door locks and safety features.

Chapter 6
Activities to Make Your Parisian Adventure Unforgettable

Paris is a city of creativity and culture, and what better way to immerse yourself in its charm than by participating in hands-on experiences and workshops? In this chapter, we will explore the diverse range of activities that Paris has to offer, from art classes and craft workshops to cooking lessons that will allow you to master the art of French cuisine. These engaging and enriching experiences will not only help you create lasting memories but also give you a deeper appreciation for the city's artistic and culinary heritage.

Hands-On Experiences and Workshops

Art Classes and Craft Workshops
Paris has been a haven for artists for centuries, and you can follow in their footsteps by taking part in art classes and craft workshops that cater to various interests and skill levels.

Painting and Drawing Classes
Unleash your inner artist with painting and drawing classes held in studios and ateliers across the city.

Whether you're a novice or have some experience with art, these classes are designed to nurture your creativity and guide you through different techniques.
Experienced instructors will teach you the fundamentals of sketching, watercolors, acrylics, and more, allowing you to capture the beauty of Paris through your artwork.

Photography Workshops
Paris is a city that beckons to be photographed, and there's no better way to improve your photography skills than by joining specialized workshops. Professional photographers will lead you on guided photo walks through the city's most photogenic spots, sharing tips on composition, lighting, and capturing the essence of Paris through your lens.

Pottery and Ceramics
For a hands-on experience with a tactile medium, consider enrolling in pottery and ceramics workshops. Discover the art of molding clay into beautiful creations, whether it's a vase, bowl, or sculpture. You'll learn the intricacies of shaping, glazing, and firing, resulting in a unique souvenir that you can take home as a cherished reminder of your time in Paris.

Jewelry Making
Craft your own personalized jewelry under the guidance of skilled artisans. Jewelry-making workshops offer an opportunity to work with various materials like beads, metals, and gemstones, allowing you to create one-of-a-kind accessories that reflect your style and taste.

Cooking Lessons: Mastering French Cuisine

French cuisine is renowned worldwide for its sophistication and delectable flavors. What better way to savor the essence of Paris than by learning the art of French cooking from experienced chefs?

Culinary Workshops

Join culinary workshops that cover a wide range of French dishes, from classic pastries to savory delicacies. These hands-on experiences take place in professional kitchens, where you'll learn essential cooking techniques, such as sautéing, baking, and sauce-making. Workshops often conclude with a delightful meal, where you can savor the fruits of your labor.

Macaron Making Classes

Macarons are delicate and colorful French pastries that have become an emblem of Parisian confectionery. Sign up for macaron-making classes, and master the art of creating these delightful treats. Learn the secrets behind the perfect meringue, piping techniques, and delectable fillings that make these sweet delicacies so irresistible.

Wine Tasting and Pairing

French cuisine is inseparable from its wine culture. Take part in wine-tasting sessions to develop your palate and gain an understanding of the diverse regions and varietals that contribute to France's rich wine heritage.

Some workshops also offer wine-pairing lessons, teaching you how to select the perfect wine to complement various dishes.

French Baking

No trip to Paris is complete without indulging in its mouth watering pastries and bread. Join a French baking class and learn the secrets of creating flaky croissants, buttery brioche, and crusty baguettes. You'll gain insights into the precise techniques required for achieving these iconic French delights.

Cheese Tasting and Pairing

Cheese is an integral part of French gastronomy, and Paris boasts a wealth of fromageries with an impressive selection of cheeses. Participate in cheese-tasting workshops where you can sample a variety of cheeses, learn about their production, and discover the art of pairing them with wine and accompaniments.

Market Tours and Cooking Classes

Embark on a culinary journey with market tours that allow you to source fresh and local ingredients. Follow this with cooking classes, where you'll transform your market finds into delectable dishes, all under the guidance of experienced chefs.

Chocolate Workshops

For chocolate lovers, Paris is a dream come true. Delight in chocolate-making workshops where you'll gain insight into the art of tempering, molding, and creating pralines and truffles. Savor the aroma and flavors as you craft your own delicious chocolates to take home.

French Family Cooking Experience

For an authentic and intimate culinary experience, consider a French family cooking class. Participate in the preparation of a home-cooked meal alongside a local family, getting a taste of traditional recipes passed down through generations. It's an excellent way to immerse yourself in Parisian culture and cuisine.

Choosing the Right Workshop

With so many workshops and experiences to choose from, it's essential to select one that aligns with your interests and schedule. Take into account the following advice as you decide:

Research and Reviews

Look for workshops and classes with positive reviews from past participants. Online platforms and travel forums are excellent resources for gathering feedback and recommendations.

Skill Level and Experience

Check if the workshop caters to your skill level, whether you're a beginner or more advanced in the chosen activity. Some workshops offer options for customization based on individual preferences and proficiency.

Group Size and Interaction
Consider the group size of the workshop, as smaller groups often allow for more personalized instruction and interaction with the instructor.

Language
Check if the workshop is conducted in a language you understand or if translation services are provided. Language barriers can impact your ability to fully participate and enjoy the experience.

Schedule and Duration
Review the schedule and duration of the workshop to ensure it fits well with your travel itinerary.

6.2

Enjoying the Outdoors: Parks, Gardens, and Picnics

Paris is not only a city of iconic landmarks and cultural treasures; it also boasts an abundance of beautiful parks, gardens, and scenic spots where you can embrace the beauty of nature. In this chapter, we will explore the many opportunities for enjoying the outdoors in Paris, from relaxing in picturesque parks to savoring a delightful picnic with a view. These outdoor experiences offer a refreshing and tranquil escape from the hustle and bustle of the city, allowing you to immerse yourself in the natural charm that Paris has to offer.

Relaxing in Parisian Parks

Luxembourg Gardens (Jardin du Luxembourg)

The Luxembourg Gardens, located in the 6th arrondissement, is one of Paris's most famous and beloved parks. Designed in the 17th century for Marie de' Medici, the gardens exude elegance and serenity. Stroll along tree-lined pathways, admire the neatly manicured lawns, and take in the beauty of the flowerbeds.

The park features a central basin with model sailboats, which visitors of all ages can rent and sail on the water. The stunning Medici Fountain provides a charming backdrop for relaxation and contemplation. Don't forget to explore the serene orchard and greenhouse, home to a delightful collection of exotic plants.

Parc des Buttes-Chaumont

The Parc des Buttes-Chaumont, located in the 19th arrondissement, is a hidden gem loved by locals and visitors alike. This hilly park offers stunning views of the city, with its rugged landscape, waterfalls, and a picturesque lake. Cross the suspension bridge to reach the central island, where a majestic temple sits atop a rocky outcrop.

The park's winding paths and hidden alcoves make it an ideal spot for a leisurely stroll or a peaceful moment of reflection. It's also a great place to have a picnic with friends or simply bask in the beauty of nature.

Parc Monceau

Parc Monceau, situated in the 8th arrondissement, is a romantic and charming park characterized by its English garden style. The park features a collection of elegant statues, pavilions, and architectural elements, creating a picturesque setting for leisure and relaxation.

With its carefully designed landscape, Parc Monceau offers a sense of tranquility and escape from the city's busy streets. Take a leisurely walk among the curved paths, admire the beautiful flowerbeds, and find a bench to sit and admire the surroundings.

Bois de Vincennes

If you crave a vast green expanse to explore, head to the Bois de Vincennes, located in the eastern outskirts of Paris. This massive park is perfect for nature lovers, offering forests, lakes, and sprawling lawns. It's a fantastic place for hiking, cycling, and engaging in various outdoor activities.

Within the Bois de Vincennes, you'll find the Parc Floral de Paris, a beautifully landscaped garden that hosts concerts and events during the summer months. The park's enchanting rose garden, themed gardens, and children's playground make it a popular spot for families and picnickers.

Scenic Picnic Spots with a View

Champ de Mars
The Champ de Mars is the vast green space that stretches out from the Eiffel Tower, making it a prime picnic spot with a front-row view of this iconic monument. Spread out a picnic blanket and indulge in a French-inspired feast while gazing up at the Eiffel Tower's majestic iron lattice.

Seine Riverbanks
The banks of the Seine River offer a romantic setting for a waterside picnic. Choose a spot along the river, such as near Pont des Arts or Pont de la Tournelle, and enjoy the gentle flow of the Seine as you savor delicious French treats.

Parc des Buttes-Chaumont Island
The central island in Parc des Buttes-Chaumont provides a unique and secluded location for a picnic. Enjoy your meal while surrounded by lush greenery and the park's enchanting landscape.

Square du Vert-Galant
This small park, situated on the western tip of the Île de la Cité, offers a peaceful oasis with stunning views of the Seine and the bridges that cross it. It's an ideal spot

for a tranquil picnic while basking in the romantic ambiance of the city.

Tips for a Perfect Picnic

Pack a Picnic Basket
Fill your picnic basket with an assortment of French delights, such as baguettes, cheeses, charcuterie, fresh fruits, and pastries. Don't forget a bottle of wine or sparkling water to complement your meal.

Bring a Comfortable Picnic Blanket
Choose a comfortable and spacious picnic blanket to ensure everyone has enough space to relax and enjoy the meal.

Sun Protection
Parisian summers can be quite warm, so don't forget to bring sunscreen, hats, and sunglasses to protect yourself from the sun's rays.

Waste Disposal
Be mindful of waste disposal by bringing trash bags with you and disposing of them responsibly.

Entertainment
Consider bringing a book, a deck of cards, or a Frisbee for some fun and entertainment during your picnic.

Chapter 7
Language and Travel Essentials

Bonjour! Basic French for Your Parisian Adventure

As you embark on your Parisian adventure, embracing a few basic French phrases can greatly enhance your experience and help you navigate the city with ease. While many Parisians speak English, making an effort to communicate in their native language shows respect and can lead to more enjoyable interactions. In this section, we'll provide you with essential French phrases for getting around the city and engaging in polite expressions and greetings.

Handy Phrases for Getting Around

1. Greetings and Pleasantries

- Bonjour (bohn-zhoor) - Hello/Good morning/Good afternoon
- Bonsoir (bohn-swahr) - Good evening
- Au revoir (oh reh-vwahr) - Goodbye
- Merci (mehr-see) - Thank you
- S'il vous plaît (seel voo pleh) - Please / I beg your pardon

- Excusez-moi (ehk-skew-zay mwah) - Excuse me/pardon me
- Parlez-vous anglais ? (par-lay vooz ahn-gleh?) - Do you speak English?

2. Introductions

- Je m'appelle [Your Name] (zhuh mah-pehl [your name]) - My name is [Your Name]
- Comment vous appelez-vous ? (koh-mahn voo zah-pleh voo?) - What is your name?
- Enchanté(e) (ahn-shahn-tay) - Nice to meet you

3. Asking for Help and Directions

- Où est...? (oo eh...?) - Where is...?
- Comment aller à...? (koh-mahn tah-lay ah...) - How do I get to...?
- À gauche (ah gohsh) - To the left
- À droite (ah dwaht) - To the right
- Tout droit (toot dwah) - Straight ahead
- Aidez-moi, s'il vous plaît (eh-deh mwah, seel voo pleh)
- Help me, please

4. Dining and Ordering

- Je voudrais... (zhuh voo-dreh...) - I would like...
- L'addition, s'il vous plaît (lah-dee-syon, seel voo pleh) - The check, please
- Combien ça coûte ? (kohm-byen sah koot?) - How much does this cost?

- C'est délicieux (say day-lee-see-yuh) - It's delicious

Polite Expressions and Greetings

1. Merci beaucoup (mehr-see boh-koo) - Thank you very much
Use this phrase to express your gratitude when someone has been especially helpful or kind.

2. Je vous en prie (zhuh vooz ahn pree) - You're welcome
This is a polite way to respond when someone thanks you.

3. Excusez-moi de vous déranger (ehk-skew-zay mwah duh voo day-rahn-zhay) - Excuse me for bothering you
Use this expression when you need to interrupt or ask for help from someone.

4. Pardon (pahr-dohn) - I'm sorry
If you accidentally bump into someone or need to get their attention, use "pardon" as a polite way to apologize.

5. Je suis désolé(e) (zhuh swee day-zoh-lay) - I'm sorry/ I apologize
This phrase is used when you want to apologize for something more significant.

6. Comment ça va ? (koh-mahn sah vah?) - How are you?

Use this friendly greeting to ask someone how they're doing.

7. Je vais bien, merci (zhuh veh byen, mehr-see) - I'm doing well, thank you

Respond with this phrase if you're feeling good and someone asks how you are.

8. Je ne parle pas bien français (zhuh nuh parl pah byan frahn-say) - I don't speak French very well

If you're not confident in your French language skills, use this phrase to let others know.

9. Parlez-vous lentement, s'il vous plaît ? (par-lay voo lahnt-mahn, seel voo pleh) - Could you speak slowly, please?

Ask someone to speak slowly if you're having trouble understanding them.

10. Je suis perdu(e) (zhuh swee pair-doo) - I'm lost

If you find yourself lost in the city, use this phrase to seek assistance.

7.2

Best Travel Season and Packing Tips

When planning a trip to Paris, it's essential to consider the best travel season and pack accordingly to ensure a comfortable and enjoyable experience. Paris is a city with distinct seasons, each offering its own unique charm and activities. In this chapter, we'll explore the different seasons in Paris and provide valuable packing tips to help you travel light while ensuring you have everything you need for easy exploration of the city.

Dressing for Different Seasons

Spring (March to May)
Spring in Paris is a delightful time to visit, as the city comes alive with blooming flowers and pleasant weather. However, it can be quite unpredictable, with occasional rain showers and temperature variations. Here's how to dress for spring:

- **Layers are key:** Pack lightweight sweaters, cardigans, and jackets that you can easily add or remove as the temperature fluctuates.

- **Bring an umbrella:** Don't forget to pack a compact umbrella to stay dry during spring showers.
- **Comfortable walking shoes:** Opt for comfortable walking shoes that are suitable for both rain and shine.

Summer (June to August)
Summer in Paris is warm and sunny, making it a popular time for tourists. Be ready for the potential of sporadic heatwaves. Here's how to dress for summer:

- **Light and breathable clothing:** Pack lightweight and breathable fabrics like cotton and linen to stay cool in the summer heat.
- **Sun protection:** Bring sunglasses, a wide-brimmed hat, and sunscreen to shield yourself from the strong sun.
- **Water bottle:** Stay hydrated throughout the day by carrying a refillable water bottle.

Fall (September to November)
Fall is a picturesque time to visit Paris, with beautiful autumn foliage and pleasant temperatures. However, it can also be chilly and rainy. Here's how to dress for fall:

- **Bring layers:** Pack sweaters, scarves, and a waterproof jacket to stay warm and dry during cooler days and occasional rain showers.
- **Comfortable boots:** Opt for comfortable and stylish boots suitable for walking on both wet and dry surfaces.
- **Fall accessories:** For added warmth on chilly days, think about bringing gloves and a nice hat.

Winter (December to February)
Winter in Paris can be chilly, with temperatures occasionally dropping below freezing. While the city is adorned with festive decorations, it's essential to dress appropriately. Here's how to dress for winter:

- **Warm layers:** Pack thermal clothing, sweaters, and a down jacket to stay warm during cold spells.
- **Winter accessories:** Don't forget to bring gloves, a scarf, and a hat to protect yourself from the cold.
- **Waterproof boots:** Choose waterproof and insulated boots to keep your feet dry and warm in case of snow or rain.

Packing Light for Easy Exploration

Packing light is essential when exploring Paris, as it allows you to move freely and make the most of your trip without the burden of heavy luggage. Here are some suggestions for effective packing:

Create a Packing List
Start by creating a detailed packing list, including essentials like clothing, toiletries, travel documents, and any electronics you may need.

Mix and Match Clothing
Pick apparel that is adaptable and can be combined with other pieces to create different looks. Stick to a neutral

color palette to make it easier to pair different pieces together.

Consider the Weather
Check the weather prediction for the days of your trip and pack appropriately. Be prepared for some changes in weather, even during a single day.

Pack Travel-Sized Toiletries
Opt for travel-sized toiletries to save space and avoid carrying large bottles of shampoo, conditioner, and other products.

Use Packing Cubes
Packing cubes can help you stay organized and maximize space in your luggage. Use them to separate different types of clothing and accessories.

Wear Bulky Items During Travel
If you're bringing bulkier items like a heavy jacket or boots, wear them during your travel days to free up space in your suitcase.

Leave Room for Souvenirs
Leave some empty space in your luggage to accommodate souvenirs and gifts you may want to bring back home.

Pack a Foldable Bag

Bring a foldable bag that you can use for day trips or as an extra carry-on for your return journey if you've acquired additional items.

Don't Forget Important Documents
Ensure you have all your important travel documents, including your passport, travel insurance, flight details, and accommodation reservations.

Chapter 8
Currency, Resources, and Safety Reminders

Understanding the Euro and Currency Exchange

Before embarking on your Parisian adventure, it's essential to understand the currency used in France and how to handle money during your trip. France is part of the Eurozone, and the official currency is the Euro (€). In this section, we'll delve into the basics of the Euro, currency exchange, and budgeting tips to help you manage your finances effectively while exploring the beautiful city of Paris.

Understanding the Euro

The Euro is the official currency of 19 of the 27 European Union (EU) member states, including France. It is divisible into 100 smaller parts called cents (¢) and is represented by the sign "€". Euro banknotes come in various denominations, including €5, €10, €20, €50, €100, €200, and €500. Euro coins are available in values of 1 cent, 2 cents, 5 cents, 10 cents, 20 cents, 50 cents, €1, and €2.

Currency Exchange

When visiting France, you'll need to exchange your home currency for Euros to make purchases and payments. Here are some essential tips for handling currency exchange:

Exchange Rates
The value of one currency in respect to another is determined by exchange rates. They fluctuate based on various factors, including economic conditions and geopolitical events. Before your trip, research the current exchange rate for your home currency to Euros. Keep in mind that exchange rates at banks and currency exchange offices may vary, so it's a good idea to compare rates to get the best deal.

Where to Exchange Money
You can exchange money at banks, currency exchange offices, or even at some hotels. Banks often offer competitive rates, but they may charge higher fees than specialized currency exchange offices. Avoid exchanging money at airports, as they typically have less favorable rates.

Notify Your Bank
Before traveling to Paris, inform your bank of your travel plans to avoid any issues with using your credit or debit cards abroad. Some banks may freeze your account

temporarily if they detect suspicious transactions in a foreign country.

ATMs in Paris
Using ATMs (Automatic Teller Machines) is a convenient way to withdraw Euros while in Paris. Look for ATMs that belong to reputable banks to ensure secure transactions. Be aware that your home bank may charge international transaction fees for using foreign ATMs.

Budgeting for Your Paris Trip

Budgeting is a crucial aspect of travel planning. Here are some tips to help you create a realistic budget for your Parisian adventure:

Accommodation
Research accommodation options that fit your budget and travel preferences. Paris offers a range of lodging choices, from luxury hotels to budget-friendly hostels and charming boutique accommodations. When making a choice, take into account elements like location, amenities, and reviews.

Food and Dining
Sampling delicious French cuisine is an essential part of your Paris experience. While dining at high-end restaurants can be a treat, also explore local cafes and street food for more budget-friendly options. Look for fixed-price menus (prix fixe) offered during lunch hours,

which often provide a more affordable way to enjoy French meals.

Sightseeing and Activities
Make a list of the main attractions and activities you want to experience in Paris. Many popular landmarks, like the Eiffel Tower and Louvre, have entrance fees. Look for discounted tickets for students or teens to save on admission costs. Additionally, take advantage of free attractions like parks, gardens, and churches.

Transportation
Consider purchasing a Paris Pass or a Paris Visite travel card for unlimited access to public transportation, including buses, trams, and the metro. This can be more cost-effective than buying individual tickets for each journey.

Shopping and Souvenirs
Set aside a specific budget for shopping and souvenirs. Paris is known for its fashion boutiques, local markets, and charming souvenir shops. Be mindful of your spending and prioritize items that hold sentimental value.

Emergency Funds
Always have a contingency fund in case of unexpected expenses or emergencies during your trip. It's wise to carry a mix of cash and cards for greater financial flexibility.

8.2

Resources and Additional Information

As a teen traveler exploring the enchanting city of Paris, having access to useful resources and information is essential for a smooth and enjoyable trip. In this chapter, we'll provide you with a comprehensive list of websites and apps specially curated for teen travelers. Additionally, we'll share important safety tips and reminders to ensure that your Parisian adventure is secure and worry-free.

Useful Websites and Apps for Teen Travelers

Google Maps
Google Maps is an invaluable tool for navigating Paris's streets, metro stations, and landmarks. The app provides real-time directions, estimated travel times, and information on public transportation options. You can even download offline maps to use when you don't have an internet connection.

CityMapper
CityMapper is another excellent navigation app that offers detailed public transportation information, including bus, metro, and walking routes. It also

provides real-time updates on transport disruptions, ensuring that you can easily find alternative routes.

Duolingo
Enhance your French language skills with Duolingo. This interactive language learning app offers fun lessons and exercises to help you master essential phrases and vocabulary before and during your trip to Paris.

Yelp
Use Yelp to discover the best restaurants, cafes, and hangout spots in Paris. Read reviews and ratings from locals and other travelers to find hidden gems and popular hotspots that suit your preferences.

Culture Trip
Culture Trip is a fantastic resource for discovering unique cultural experiences, events, and local customs in Paris. The app offers curated articles and recommendations to immerse yourself in the city's vibrant culture.

Parisianist
Parisianist is a go-to app for finding trendy and offbeat places loved by Parisians. Explore local boutiques, restaurants, and attractions that may not be on the typical tourist radar.

Time Out Paris
Stay up to date with the latest events, exhibitions, and entertainment options in Paris with Time Out Paris. The

app provides comprehensive listings and reviews for all types of activities.

RER and Metro Apps
Download apps like RATP and Next Stop Paris to access up-to-date information on RER and metro schedules, stations, and service disruptions.

Visit Paris by Metro
This app is specifically designed to guide you through Paris using the metro system. It features detailed metro maps and station information to help you get around the city efficiently.

10. GoEuro
GoEuro is a helpful app for planning trips beyond Paris. It allows you to compare and book trains, buses, and flights to explore other cities and countries in Europe.

Safety Tips and Reminders for a Secure Trip

Be Aware of Your Surroundings
Always be aware of your surroundings and stay alert, especially in crowded tourist areas and public transportation.

Keep Your Valuables Secure
Keep your valuables, such as passport, money, and electronics, secure in a money belt or a lockable bag. Avoid carrying large amounts of cash.

Use Hotel Safes

If your accommodation offers a safe, use it to store your passport and other valuables when you're not using them.

Stay Connected

Ensure that you have access to a working phone or internet connection to stay in touch with your travel companions and family back home.

Emergency Contacts

Save important contact numbers, including local emergency services and your country's embassy or consulate, in your phone.

Avoid Revealing Your Accommodation

Avoid sharing specific details about your accommodation with strangers to protect your privacy and security.

Stay with Your Group

If you're traveling with a group, stick together, especially during nighttime or in unfamiliar areas.

Respect Local Laws and Customs

Familiarize yourself with local laws and customs to ensure that you stay on the right side of the law and respect the culture of the city.

Travel Insurance

Consider purchasing travel insurance to provide financial protection in case of unforeseen events or emergencies.

Stay Informed

Stay informed about any potential safety risks or travel advisories for Paris during your trip.

Conclusion

As we bid adieu to the City of Lights, it's time to reflect on the incredible journey we've taken together through the pages of this book.

Throughout our exploration, you've witnessed the grandeur of iconic landmarks like the Eiffel Tower and the Louvre, and ventured into the hidden nooks and crannies that make Paris truly unique. You've indulged in delectable pastries, mastered the art of café culture, and embraced the warmth of the Parisian spirit.

As we navigate the city's bustling streets, you've grown familiar with its culture and customs, immersing yourself in the legacy of artists, writers, and visionaries who have shaped this city into an eternal muse for creativity and innovation.

And as you leave a piece of your heart behind in the cobbled streets and charming alleyways, know that Paris will forever hold a place in your soul. The memories you've made here, the laughter shared, and the experiences lived will forever be cherished, shaping your perspective on the world and igniting a sense of wanderlust within you.

But this is not goodbye; rather, it's a "à bientôt," and until we meet again. For Paris will always be here, waiting to welcome you back with open arms whenever you choose to return.

As you journey on from the City of Lights, carry the spirit of Paris with you. Let the lessons learned, the art admired, and the history absorbed be the foundation for your future adventures, inspiring you to explore new horizons with curiosity and an open heart.

And so, as we close the final chapter of this book, remember that this is just the beginning of a lifetime of exploration and discovery. Keep the magic of Paris alive within you, and may it forever fuel your desire to wander, to seek new experiences, and to embrace the beauty of the world around you.

Au revoir, dear traveler, until we meet again under the twinkling lights of Paris or in the captivating embrace of another extraordinary destination. Safe travels, and may your adventures continue to be filled with wonder and joy. Bon voyage!

Printed in Great Britain
by Amazon

38210619R00069